Filling My Empty Nest With Good Things:

The Challenges of Mommy Retirement

By D. M. Warsalla

Your child has moved out and left the house. Everything seems to have suddenly come to a grinding halt. No more running kids for doctor visits, physicals and dental exams, and orthodontist appointments. No more school sports, conferences and other functions to attend.

When my children were younger, I thought "wait stop this merry-go-round, so I can get off. Now that merry-go-round has stopped, and I wanted back on . How we used too long for the day the kids would leave so we could have a moment to ourselves, only to awaken from our daydream to change diapers, fold laundry and cook meals. Where did all the time go? They were little and now they are grown! Now those days are gone. The house is so quiet you can hear a pin drop. You would give anything for those noisy, busy days to be back caring for your children.

In the beginning of mommy retirement, we walk around in shock about how much and how fast our life has changed since our last baby flew the coop and left the nest, and they were so happy about it!

We once hated the time our teens would spend on their cell phones, now we thank God for them so we aren't waiting by the phone at home for our children to call us, because it could be a very long time.

Sometimes the empty nest can be like someone turned the light switch off and it only comes back on when our children call or visit us. Of course, we love to see our kids but there is life in between visits, our new life.

For stay-at-home moms I think the empty nest is the hardest because our identities are so wrapped up in being a mom to our children. Homeschooling moms who have been with their children 24/7 and sacrificed much mommy retirement can affect them the most.

Single moms and those moms who have worked outside the home may have regrets. They may have missed much of their child's growing up and can especially have a difficult time with the challenge of mommy retirement. Some women are entering both job and mommy retirement experiencing them simultaneously. This can be especially challenging.

While we love our children and want them to grow up being happy successful adults, we also wish they didn't grow up and leave us. Sometimes our young adult children will need to come back to finish college or find a new job or career. At first, we are elated but then reality sets in. Adult children who have been on their own do not want to be told what to do by their mom. But they do need to respect your home and house rules. It's a good thing to have them sign a contract with house rules stated before they moved back, and even then, be prepared for rules to be broken. This can cause conflict and then we understand why baby birds are kicked out of the nest and forced to learn to fly on their own.

We need to love our children enough to set them free into the cold, cruel world believing in them and believing they will learn to fly. When a baby bird is learning to fly, they are called fledglings. They fall out of the nest, hop and flap their wings trying to fly. This strengthens their wing muscles so eventually they will be able to fly. The mother bird is usually close by watching over her fledglings and stooping down on predators.

Back to the shock factor we experience when they leave our home. We have prepared them for this day and everything has been for this purpose. When the day finally comes, we wish it never came. Truthfully, we didn't think this day would ever come.

Leaving the nest would never come if teenagers weren't hormonal-sassy messes. Teenagers stress out their parents with all the experimentation they do. Fighting and arguing about everything under the sun. They want their autonomy and freedom. This helps us be able to push them out of the nest.

Married ladies one note about your husband. They have seen this day, and they rejoice. They are not as emotionally upset or sad about this. To them it means a new chapter in their life with you all to themselves. I was shocked at how quickly my husband wanted them to fly away! Our husbands are here to help us cut the umbilical cords yet once again.

Our husband's identity is his job while our identity has been in being a mother. If a father is the main caregiver of his children, he will be more emotionally invested in his children. Leaving the nest will have a greater impact on him.

All kidding aside, we are emotionally more complex than a bird. Mommy retirement can be tough. For some mothers it might take longer to adjust to this major change. It's more like forced retirement. Our children turn 18 and they want to leave, while others leave around twenty- one. Our children just become adults. I have been there, and I understand the pain and confusion you are experiencing deep in your heart. I wrote this journal to help you navigate through this difficult time in your life. No one will ever know or experience the depth of your pain, except another mother who has gone through the empty nest. It's good to talk to another mother who has gone through this transition.

It's normal to be a little depressed, cry and mourn for your changing role in your children's lives. This is a major change and can affect you deeply. We can go through the 5 stages of grief defined by Elizabeth Kubler Ross. They are Denial (shocked, hard to believe), Depression, anger (regret too), bargaining (trying to guilt our adult children into visiting), and finally acceptance (we move on with our life). Whenever there is a major change or transition in our lives such as the death of a loved one, divorce, moving away from family, loss of job or status, a loss of any kind can cause us to grieve that loss.

When our children do not call or visit, we may view this as rejection. The truth is, our children are out in the world working and having relationships that don't include us. This can be difficult for us as moms to understand because they have always been with us every day (unless a divorced parent has no visitation rights). It is important to realize your children are not rejecting you.

Another issue that can affect how we feel is menopause and hormone imbalance. Lack of energy can occur making us feel tired and add to depression. It is important to take care of our bodies with proper nutrition, vitamins, mineral and herbs to balance hormones. Exercise such as walking, and swimming, helps increase our mood.

One of the major adjustments I had was the peace and quiet. There were so many times while my kids were young, I longed for peace and quiet. When I finally got it, it took a lot of getting used too. The quiet was unnerving at first. I wanted to fill the quiet with noise. The TV on or radio playing. Eventually I learned to love it. In fact, one of my grandkids mentioned how quiet it was at my place.

Another major realization came and I experienced shock at not knowing who I was apart from my children. I remember saying to myself, "Who am I. Now, what am I supposed to do?" It took a while for me to discover who I was apart from my children.

Learning to cook smaller meals was a big adjustment. I would cook all my meals for a couple weeks in one day and freeze them. Instead of vacuuming once a week, I vacuumed one a month! I only used my dishwasher once a week instead of everyday. I did laundry once every two weeks instead of everyday. Washed the floors and cleaned bathrooms once a month. I saved time and money.

I wrote this journal to help you with the challenge of mommy retirement. You will always be your child's mother, but the definition of mommy has changed. Your child is no longer dependent upon you to help them make decisions, make choices for them, or anything at all.

Writing down your difficulties during this major transition can help you identify where you are struggling and help you make changes and discover a better way.

Establishing a new routine can help us remember to eat and groom ourselves. We had a very different routine with our children. Maybe you still want to keep it, or you want to sleep in later and stay up later. It's important to take care of yourself. Changes in our daily routine can take us off balance until we start a new routine and do it every day until it becomes automatic. Make a schedule keep a planner. Maybe you don't have much to do, but put it down anyway.

Not only can we be in a state of shock when reality sets in and out last child has flown the coop, we can also receive a double whammy when we realize we don't know who we are. We may have no one to take care of and our identity was in being a mom. Panic can set in as we realize we don't know who we are apart from our children. We don't have to fear this but explore and discover new things about ourselves.

Some moms can stay in the grieving stage never understanding how to get out of it. Learning how to live our lives past our children is important for our mental health and enjoying our lives. We love to see our children, but we have a life in between visits, our new life! We realize, we are embarking on a new life with new possibilities.

We can rekindle the romance in our marriage, with no interruptions – Wow! We can go to college earn a degree, learn a trade or career, travel, join the work force, volunteer, join a club, learn a new hobby, get a pedicure, the possibilities are endless. We can start a new life and look forward to waking up every day as we discover who we are and explore new things.

It is my hope this journal helps you recognize who you are apart from your children. You can purposely choose to enjoy your new life exploring and experiencing new things and learning to fill your empty nest with good things.

 You will get through this and come out the other side learning who you are, realizing you have met the challenge of mommy retirement, and start a new chapter in your life knowing there is life after the empty nest and it is full of good things!

Wait for the grandkids!!! It's only a little time before grandkids come along, so enjoy your quiet time while you can! Being a grandparent is 10 times better than being a parent. If you don't have grandchildren adopt a family who doesn't have a grandma or one nearby. Bake, babysit, and have a blast.

How to use this Journal

- You can answer each prompt in order or out of order
- You can choose to answer prompt questions or not
- You can skip the prompts altogether
- This journal is about your journey

I would like to hear from you about how this journal has helped you.
Joylady2012@gmail.com

Please leave an awesome review on Amazon.
   Other Journals on Amazon:

My Songwriting Guitar Journal
My Songwriting Piano Journal
My Weather Prayer Journal

How has my routine changed?

If I don't like my routine I can change it

Create a new routine for yourself

How has the empty nest affected me?How have my meals changed?

Plan my meals for one to two weeks. Cook and freeze them

Plan my meals for one to two weeks. Cook and freeze them

How are chores and cleaning different?

I have time to do...

Pros to my life without children living at home

Cons to my life without children living at home

With less time spent on meal preparation and cooking I will use this extra time for...

With less time spent cleaning I will use this extra time for...

With less time spent doing laundry I will use this extra time for...

How is quietness and silence affecting me?

How is quietness and silence affecting me?

If it's too quiet in the library I can go to Starbucks

If it's too quiet in the library I can go to Starbucks

When I miss my children I...

The most difficult thing is...

The most fun thing is...

What does it feel like to be able to sleep in?

What I miss most about each of my children?

Where am I in the 5 stages of grief, denial, depression, anger, bargaining, acceptance?

Do I have a friend who has gone through the empty nest to talk to about my struggles?

Today I will wipe away my tears, brush my teeth and comb my hair even if I go nowhere

Today I am going to start a new routine

Today I am getting fresh air and sunshine

My children are not rejecting me, they are living their lives as adults

Today I am going to do something I enjoy

Today I am going to have lunch at a park, lake or ocean

I promise myself I will not make my children feel guilty for missing my birthday or not visiting

Today I choose to move beyond my tears

I plan long term goals

I plan short term goals

I plan short term goals

Make a list of things I have always wanted to do but never had the time

Do one or two things I have always wanted to do

If I can't stand the quiet I can go to a noisy place like Starbucks

If I can't stand the quiet I can go to a noisy place like Starbucks

When I think about my children being gone I...

Spend some of my free time getting to know me

My favorite things are...

I have time for myself, what will I do?

I have time for myself, what will I do?

Who am I?

Who am I apart from my children?

Who do I want to be?

What I like...

What I dislike...

What good things can I fill my empty nest with?

What is my new purpose now?

What would I like to do?

Spend more time with my spouse or significant other

I am planning a romantic get-away

I am planning a romantic get-away

Today I will splurge on...

Play a game. My favorite games are...

My favorite TV shows are...

Thinking about my purpose

Read a magazine

Create a photo scrape book album

My favorite songs are...

Plan a local trip. What will I do? Who would I bring?

My favorite things to do are...

Bake something for a friend or neighbor

Invite a friend over for a special dinner

Get a pedicure or nails done or both

Find new friends, join a club

My life is starting to gravitate around me!

Besides seeing my children, I am looking forward to...

Liking my new life, how?

Start a new hobby, Go outside for a walk

Read a book

Plan annual physical with doctor

Get outside, what did you do?

Plan a short trip

Go to Starbucks with a friend

My purpose is?

My children aren't rejecting me

I resist the urge to manipulate my child into visiting me

Where am I now in the 5 stages of grief?

Learn something new

Join a club or group of people with similar interests

As I fill my empty nest with good things, what have I learned about myself?

Volunteer, or start a job

Go to college or just take a class

Join a cooking class

Learn a new job or trade

Volunteer at a school

What new thing have I learned about myself?

How am I missing my children today?

Where am I in the 5 stages of grief?

Plan another trip. Where will I go this time?

I make a difference, how?

I have regrets about my children and being there for them

If I could live my life differently, how would I?

Ride a bike, take a walk, join the YMCA

Ride a bike, take a walk, join the YMCA

How can I volunteer doing the thing I love most?

What gives my life meaning?

I am taking care of my health and balancing hormones

I am learning who I am...

I enjoy my new life...

Join a book, garden or chess club

Join a quilting club or take an art class

Go on a Senior trip with a group

Visit the zoo, museum, aquarium or art gallery

My life is filled with good things…

There is life after the empty nest...